FOR THE BROKEN

by Shenaia Lucas

this book
is my heart
in your hands

-be kind

CHAPTERS

chapter one

for the healing

he promised
she trusted
he left
she broke

*-but you are so much stronger than
that*

she was beautiful
before he said so
and she remained beautiful
when he stopped saying it

-*you are your own standard*

they never understand
what it's like to be
at rock bottom

-even though we've all been there

forget him, darling

*-he wasn't worth your attention
anyway*

he took her for granted
and lost a diamond
chasing glitter

-men can be so blind

if your love for him
broke you
your love for yourself
can heal you

-the simplest truth of healing

he wanted to drink her
like wine
but forgot that she
could drown him

-and she did

you are not
your insecurities
you are the strength
of the mountains
and the wisdom
of the rivers

you are
everything

-yourself

when you have finally
healed yourself
he will
come around again
for he is addicted
to breaking hearts

but remember, darling
remember what he is
and don't forget
what you have learned

-do not take him back

sleep tight
let your body fix itself
and your mind
repair the holes
worry left there
today

sleep tight
and fight again
tomorrow

-make time for healing

do not fear
for god is with you
he who created
heaven and earth
and sees the movements
of every sparrow
will not allow your heart
to be hurt again

-he is there for you

forget
for the moment
your brokenness

remember
for a moment
how he loves you

-god will never abandon you

do not get lost
in how broken
you feel

find your strength
in places
you never expected

-the lioness awakens

losing
what matters most
to you

is the beginning
of becoming
yourself

-and that's the beauty of it

do not close
your broken heart

open it
and let in the light

-under the sunlight we grow

love
broke your heart

love
will heal your wounds

-the circle of life

rise, warrior
you have come back
from the dead
scarred
but stronger than before

-grief is the process of being reborn

take heart
you may think
you will never
feel joy again

but winter
doesn't last forever
and the first rays
of summer light
will arrive
with the dawn
of morning.

-the morning always comes

do not despair
that you are not yet healed
and do not give up
on the process

healing will bloom
like the crops of spring
and you will feast on love
again

-the flower always blooms

you are an alchemist
turning sorrow into joy
and graves into gold

-the art of transmutation

you have given
enough time
to pain

the time
for healing
has begun

-*healing begins now*

take solace
in those
who have stood by you
through it all

loyalty
is of infinite value
and so rare
these days

remember
who was there
when you were broken
and do not forget them
in their own times
of trial

-help each other heal

you were whole
before him
and you can be whole
after him

-he does not complete you

you have bled
every month

do not let him
make you now believe
that he has won
just because
he drew
a little blood

-*we were made for this battlefield*

the last step
of healing
is to forgive

not those
who hurt you
for they
are nothing

the last step
of healing
is to forgive

yourself.

-*the healing completes*

&

chapter two

we were never
a fairy tale
we have
our imperfections
we fight
and hurt
each other

but fairy tales
end
with the last page
and our reality
never has
to end.

-the truth of the matter

i will love you
when your light
is all but snuffed out
by the darkness

i will love you
when you think
you've never been
more broken

i will love you
through it all
because you
are mine

-i will love you

your love
made the world
smell like roses

-your garden

when i don't
wake up
next to you

i wish
i hadn't woken up
at all

-you are my everything

you are
the color
of my life

without you
i would be gray

you are
the music
of my days

without you
i would prefer silence

-you are

if you don't
first fall in love
with my mind
soul
and heart

if you don't
win my trust
before you try
to get in my pants

then i don't
want you
at all.

-*the order of things*

i am grateful
for every heartbreak
i felt
before
we fell in love

for each scar
taught me a new place
to caress you

-caress

you weren't my first
but you were the first
to matter

-first

let's find again
the tree
under which
we first
fell in love

let's recreate
that one moment
because i swear to god
i've never felt
anything
so perfect

-back to the start

earth
is a funny place

for at its core
it burns
with the scorching
power
of a thousand
fires

and yet
on its surface
there is life
and water.

i will protect you
from the fires
that burn within

and i will nourish you
with a gentle touch
keeping your heart
safe

for i cannot control
what i am made of
but i can control
how i love you.

-the best parts of me are yours

if you never cried
if it never bent you
if it was never
a struggle

was it really
love?

-the real thing

in sickness
and
in health

mental
and
physical

-both

there are
a million
lovesongs

and i could
listen
to them all

thinking
of
you

-*infinity*

my father
shook the house
with his yelling

you whisper
sweet nothings
barely above silence

-you wont reopen my wounds

forget everything
all i need
is you

-run away with me

don't call me an angel
i'm not perfect
and i will hurt you
despite
my best intentions

call me human
and let us love
each other
as best
we can

-reality is sweeter

how are you?
did you sleep well?
have you eaten today?
did you drink enough water?

-tell me you love me

lust isn't love
but it sure
is part
of it

-*attraction*

seduce me
from my brain
outwards

-*instruction manual*

the best song
i ever heard
was the way
you moaned

-music

you are better
than my dreams
for when i reach out
to touch you
you smile
instead of fading
back into
my imagination

-real

you looked right past
my inadequacies
no, even better
you loved them
better
than anyone
has ever loved
the best parts
of me

-adequate

i don't need you
but i want you
and that
makes all
the difference

-true love

chapter three

for the oppressed

how is it
that women
are so much
of humanity

and yet
are treated
as so little

-*representation*

if they photoshop
their models
they're already
lying to you

-never trust a liar

i pray
that i never
become immune
to injustice

for the struggle
of any
is the struggle
of all

-desensitized

she is a woman
because she says she is
it's that simple

-identify

"she's lying
she wants attention
she's a whore
she led him on
she regretted it
it's her fault"

*-and they wonder why we don't
speak out*

feminism
that is only
for white women
isn't feminism
at all

-we are all in this together

our culture
worships musicians
who brag
about date rape
in their songs

our country
elects politicians
who brag
about sexual assault
and face
no consequences

there
is something
seriously wrong
with this
picture

-the system is stacked against us

when the poor
can't afford
justice

we are not
a democracy
we are
an oligarchy

-tilted scales

if you only
denounce evil
and do nothing
about it

you are part
of the problem

-problem

they were willing
to tear the country
apart

just to stop
a black man
from leaving
the legacy
he could have

-*the audacity of being black*

it's her body
it's her choice
end of discussion

-her choice

they say
they want to
protect
the innocent unborn

yet as soon
as it is born
they want
to let it die

-supposedly pro-life

the future
is female,
diverse,
equal,
and all the better
for it

-a matter of time

who they worship
what they wear
and the book they read
does not
make them
terrorists

-end profiling

just because
you have free speech
doesn't mean
there will be
no consequences
for spewing
hate speech

*-just because you can doesn't mean
you should*

white people
are so unaccustomed
to giving up power
that they go insane
at being told
that one single word
is not theirs
to use

-it's not that hard

if you really believe
that history
is as white and male
as they wrote it
in those books
you are a fool

-not just his story

they want
to take food
out of the mouths
of hungry children

because apparently
they just can't live
without
another yacht

-*welfare*

they were born
next to the finish line
of this race
and yet
refuse
to acknowledge
the advantage
they obtained
with their
first breath

-*white privilege*

where's the justice
in a life sentence
for growing a plant
that should be
legal anyway?

-legalize justice

millions of children
without a family
and our government
would rather
those children die
or grow up alone
than let
queer people
give them families

-they'd rather burn the house in
winter than let others find shelter in
it

when viagra
must be covered
but birth control
is a burden
you know
who's making
the rules

-we need more women in power

they want to keep
their monuments
to slave-owning traitors
and fly the flag
of our enemies
because they can't accept
that their superiority
began to slowly die
when the flyers
of that flag
lost

-sore losers

they will go
to such incredible lengths
to hate

-battle

men
need to learn
to take no
for an answer

-teach them young

fight
for the oppressed
for the fight
of any
is the fight
of all

-for the oppressed

chapter four

for the broken

the darkness
will not last
forever

-*wait for morning*

love is powerful
but
do not be fooled;
it will fix nothing
by itself

-elixir

your brokenness
is beautiful

not because
of the way you are

but because
of the way
you will be
when you are finally
free

-a phoenix in waiting

pain has always been there
when love abandoned me

because i never
quite figured out
how to break it off

-*pain remains*

the season
will pass
as it
always
has

-*fate*

your wounds
will scar
and you will be
stronger
than before

-power

it's hard to heal
when
your mind
has moved on
but your heart
is stuck
in the past

-the heart is a slow learner

if you never forget
the darkness
of the past
you can never
make space
for the light
of
the present

-move aside

you
are stronger
than you know

you
think
you're at
your limits
but you
are not
even close

you only see
the tip
of the iceberg

but deep within
you are more
than you seem

you are stronger
than you ever
could have
imagined

-*stronger*

you would
have done
anything
for him

but now
it's time
to learn
to do
everything
without
him

-*death of intentions*

let go
of safety

you will
survive
the fall

-made of steel

never
let anyone
make you
believe
you are not
enough

you
are.

-you are enough

you are not
a damsel
in distress

you are
the dragon

and the world
had better
be ready

-the dragon

let
the past
die

let
the future
bloom

-*bloom*

don't
blame
yourself

not
this time

-blame

reinvent
yourself
from the ashes

build
a skyscraper
from the dirt

-upwards

you look into the crowd
looking for a face
who understands

who feels
like the world
is crumbling
like you do

you feel alone
—and you are—
but you
are all
you need

-*sorrow in solitude*

she is a shadow
of her past self

a shadow
where her scars
can't be seen

but she
will not stay
that way

she
was meant
for the light

-*shadow*

she has shattered
for the thousandth time
but
for the thousandth time
she
will piece herself
back together

-again and again

we are all
broken

and yet
we endure

-human

you are
broken
beyond all hope
poured out
past your limits
and yet
still giving
to others

for you
are the dawn
of a love
that never
gives up

-*you will never give up*

this
is a message
to the broken

you
may feel
that everything
has ended
the world
has collapsed
and there is nothing
worth living for

but hold on
you will feel joy
again

-for the broken

the end.

Made in the USA
San Bernardino, CA
29 August 2017